Opa's Christmas Cookies

JESSICA KOENIG

Brooklyn, New York
2025

Copyright © 2025 Jessica Koenig

All rights reserved. No part of this book may be reproduced, stored, or transmitted in any form or by any means without written permission from the author, except for brief quotations used in reviews.

First printing, 2025.

ISBN: 979-8-9990336-8-0

Butter Cookies	7
Oatmeal Cookies	8
Black & White Cookies	9
Sugar Cookie Dough	10
Spritz	11
Drop Nut Cookies	12
Walnut Crescents	13
Peanut Butter Oatmeal Cookies	15
Snickerdoodles	16
Peanut Butter Oatmeal Cookies	17
Easy Candied Nuts	18
Chocolate Almond Cookies	19
Buttery Oatmeal Crisps	20
Brown Sugar Nut Drops	21
Lebkuchen	22
Pfeffernüsse	24
Linzer Cookies	25
Shortbread Cookies	26
Gingerbread Cookies	27
Coconut Macaroons	28
Biscotti (Almond or Chocolate Chip)	29
Vanillekipferl	30
Italian Ricotta Cookies	31
Thumbprint Jam Cookies	32
Snowball Cookies	33

Butter Cookies

Yield: about 24 cookies

Ingredients:
- 1 *c* butter, softened
- 1 *c* sugar
- 2 eggs
- 1 *tsp* vanilla
- 1 *tsp* baking powder
- 3 *c* flour
- pinch of salt

Method:
- Preheat oven to 350°F.
- In a bowl, cream butter and sugar until light and fluffy.
- Add eggs and vanilla; mix until combined.
- In a separate bowl, whisk flour, baking powder, and salt.
- Add dry ingredients to butter mixture and mix until dough forms.
- Shape, roll, or cut as desired.
- Place on baking sheet and bake 8–10 min or until edges are lightly golden.

Oatmeal Cookies

Yield: about 24 cookies

Ingredients:
- 1 *c* butter
- 1 *c* sugar
- 1 *c* brown sugar
- 2 eggs
- 1 *tsp* vanilla
- 1½ *c* flour
- 1 *tsp* baking soda
- ½ *tsp* salt
- 3 *c* oats
- optional:
    - 1 *c* raisins or chocolate chips

Method:
- Preheat oven to 350°F.
- Cream butter, sugar, and brown sugar.
- Add eggs and vanilla; mix well.
- Whisk flour, baking soda, and salt together.
- Add dry ingredients to bowl and mix until combined.
- Stir in oats and raisins or chocolate chips if using.
- Drop spoonfuls onto sheet and bake 10–12 min.

Black & White Cookies

Yield: about 24 cookies

Ingredients:
- ½ *c* butter
- 1 *c* sugar
- 2 eggs
- 1½ *c* flour
- ½ *tsp* baking soda
- ½ *tsp* salt
- ½ *c* cocoa (for half the dough)
- 1 *tsp* vanilla

Method:
- Preheat oven to 350°F.
- Cream butter and sugar until fluffy.
- Add eggs and vanilla; mix until combined.
- Whisk flour, baking soda, and salt; add to mixture.
- Divide dough in half; mix cocoa into one half.
- Roll each dough into ropes; twist together.
- Slice cookies and arrange on baking sheet.
- Bake 10–12 min.

Sugar Cookie Dough

Yield: about 24 cookies

Ingredients:

- 1 *lb* butter
- 2 *c* sugar
- 4 eggs
- 4 *c* flour

Method:

- Preheat oven to 350°F.
- Cream butter and sugar.
- Add eggs one at a time.
- Add flour gradually until dough forms.
- Chill dough 1 hour.
- Roll out, cut shapes, place on sheet.
- Bake 8–10 min.

Spritz

Yield: about 24 cookies

Ingredients:
- ¾ c butter
- ½ c sugar
- 1 egg
- 2 c flour
- ¼ *tsp* salt
- ½ *tsp* vanilla or almond extract

Method:
- Preheat oven to 350°F.
- Cream butter and sugar until smooth.
- Add egg and extract; mix well.
- Add flour and salt; mix until dough forms.
- Load dough into cookie press.
- Press shapes onto ungreased sheet.
- Bake 8–10 min.

Drop Nut Cookies

Yield: about 24 cookies

Ingredients:
- 5 *oz* almond paste
- ½ *c* sugar
- 8 *oz* butter
- 1 egg
- 5 *oz* flour
- 1 *tsp* baking powder
- cinnamon sugar (for tops)

Method:
- Preheat oven to 350°F.
- Blend almond paste, sugar, and butter until smooth.
- Add egg and mix well.
- Whisk flour and baking powder; add to dough.
- Drop spoonfuls of dough onto sheet.
- Roll tops in cinnamon sugar.
- Bake until edges are golden.

Toasted Almond White Chocolate Chip Cookies

Yield: about 24 cookies

Ingredients:
- ½ *c* butter
- ½ *c* sugar
- ½ *c* brown sugar
- 1 egg
- 1½ *tsp* almond extract
- 1½ *c* flour
- ½ *tsp* baking soda
- ½ *tsp* salt
- 1 *c* white chocolate chips
- 1 *c* toasted almonds

Method:
- Preheat oven to 350°F.
- Cream butter, sugar, and brown sugar.
- Add egg and almond extract; mix well.
- Whisk flour, baking soda, and salt; add to bowl.
- Stir in white chocolate chips and almonds.
- Drop spoonfuls onto sheet.
- Bake 10–12 min.

Walnut Crescents

Yield: about 24 cookies

Ingredients:
- 1 *c* butter
- ½ *c* powdered sugar
- 2 *tsp* vanilla
- 2 *c* flour
- 1 *c* finely chopped walnuts

Method:
- Preheat oven to 350°F.
- Cream butter and powdered sugar.
- Add vanilla and mix.
- Add flour and walnuts; mix until dough forms.
- Roll dough into thin ropes and shape into crescents.
- Bake 10–12 min.
- Dust with powdered sugar while warm.

Peanut Butter Oatmeal Cookies

Yield: about 24 cookies

Ingredients:
- ½ *c* butter
- ½ *c* sugar
- ½ *c* brown sugar
- 1 egg
- 1 *c* peanut butter
- 1 *tsp* vanilla
- 1 *tsp* baking soda
- ½ *tsp* salt
- 1 *c* flour
- 1½ *c* oats
- optional:
    - chocolate chips

Method:

- Preheat oven to 350°F.
- Cream butter, sugar, and brown sugar.
- Add egg, peanut butter, and vanilla; mix well.
- Whisk flour, baking soda, and salt; mix in.
- Stir in oats (+ chips if using).
- Drop dough onto sheet.
- Bake 10–12 min.

Snickerdoodles

Yield: about 24 cookies

Ingredients:
- ½ *c* butter
- ¾ *c* sugar
- 1 egg
- 1½ *c* flour
- 1 *tsp* baking powder
- ½ *tsp* baking soda
- 1 *tsp* cream of tartar
- ¼ *tsp* salt
- coating:
    - 2 *tbsp* sugar
    - 2 *tsp* cinnamon

Method:
- Preheat oven to 350°F.
- Cream butter and sugar.
- Add egg; mix well.
- Whisk flour, baking powder, baking soda, tartar, and salt.
- Add dry ingredients to bowl.
- Roll dough into balls.
- Coat in cinnamon-sugar mixture.
- Bake 10 min.

Heidesand

Yield: about 24 cookies

Ingredients:
- 1 *c* butter
- ¾ *c* sugar
- 2 *tsp* vanilla
- 2 *c* flour
- ¼ *tsp* salt
- optional:
    - coarse sugar for rolling

Method:
1. Melt butter in a saucepan and cook until lightly browned; cool completely.
2. Preheat oven to 350°F.
3. Mix browned butter and sugar until smooth.
4. Add vanilla, then flour and salt; mix into a soft dough.
5. Shape dough into a log and chill 1 hour.
6. Slice into rounds (roll edges in coarse sugar if desired).
7. Arrange on baking sheet.
8. Bake 10–12 min or until lightly golden.

Candied Nuts

Yield: about 2 cups nuts

Ingredients:
- 2 *c* mixed nuts
- ½ *c* sugar
- ¼ *c* brown sugar
- 1 *tsp* cinnamon
- ¼ *tsp* salt
- 1 egg white
- 1 *tsp* water or vanilla

Method:
- Preheat oven to 300°F.
- Whisk egg white and water until frothy.
- Add nuts and coat evenly.
- Mix sugar, brown sugar, cinnamon, and salt.
- Toss nuts in sugar mixture.
- Spread on lined sheet.
- Bake 25–30 min, stirring halfway.

Chocolate Almond Cookies

Yield: about 24 cookies

Ingredients:
- 1 *c* butter
- 1 *c* sugar
- 1 *c* brown sugar
- 2 eggs
- 1 *tsp* almond extract
- 1 *tsp* vanilla
- 2¼ *c* flour
- ½ *c* cocoa
- 1 *tsp* baking soda
- ½ *tsp* salt
- 1 *c* chopped almonds
- optional:
    - 1 *c* chocolate chips

Method:
- Preheat oven to 350°F.
- Cream butter, sugar, and brown sugar.
- Add eggs, almond extract, and vanilla.
- Whisk flour, cocoa, baking soda, and salt; add to bowl.
- Stir in almonds (+ chips if using).
- Drop dough onto sheet.
- Bake 10–12 min.

Buttery Oatmeal Crisps

Yield: about 24 cookies

Ingredients:
- 1 *c* melted butter
- 1 *c* sugar
- 1 *c* brown sugar
- 2 eggs
- 1 *tsp* vanilla
- 1½ *c* flour
- 1 *tsp* baking soda
- ½ *tsp* salt
- 3 *c* oats

Method:
- Preheat oven to 350°F.
- Mix melted butter, sugar, and brown sugar.
- Add eggs and vanilla; mix well.
- Whisk flour, baking soda, and salt; add to bowl.
- Stir in oats.
- Drop tiny spoonfuls onto sheet (they spread a lot).
- Bake 8–10 min.

Brown Sugar Nut Drops

Yield: about 24 cookies

Ingredients:
- ½ *c* butter
- 1 *c* brown sugar
- 1 egg
- 1 *tsp* vanilla
- 1½ *c* flour
- 1 *tsp* baking powder
- ¼ *tsp* salt
- ½ *c* milk
- 1 *c* chopped nuts

Method:
- Preheat oven to 350°F.
- Cream butter and brown sugar.
- Add egg and vanilla.
- Whisk flour, baking powder, and salt.
- Add dry ingredients alternately with milk.
- Stir in nuts.
- Drop dough onto sheet.
- Bake 10–12 min.

Lebkuchen

Yield: about 24 cookies

Ingredients:
- ½ *c* honey
- ½ *c* molasses
- ¾ *c* brown sugar
- 1 egg
- 1 *tbsp* lemon juice
- 1 *tsp* lemon zest
- 2½ *c* flour
- 1 *tsp* baking soda
- 1 *tsp* cinnamon
- 1 *tsp* ginger
- ½ *tsp* nutmeg
- ½ *tsp* cloves
- ½ *tsp* allspice
- ½ *tsp* salt
- ½ *c* finely chopped nuts (almonds or hazelnuts)
- optional:
    - ½ *c* candied citrus peel, finely chopped
- Glaze:
    - 1 *c* powdered sugar
    - 2 *tbsp* milk or water

Method:
- In a saucepan, warm honey and molasses over low heat until thin and smooth. Remove from heat.
- Stir in brown sugar and cool slightly.
- Add egg, lemon juice, and lemon zest; mix well.
- In a separate bowl, whisk flour, baking soda, spices, and salt.
- Add dry ingredients to molasses mixture and mix into a soft dough.
- Stir in nuts (and candied peel if using).
- Chill dough for at least 1 hour.
- Preheat oven to 350°F.
- Roll dough into balls or press into rounds.
- Bake 10–12 min until lightly firm.
- While warm, brush with glaze if desired.
- Cool on a rack and rest 1-2 days.

Chocolate Chip Cookies

Yield: about 24 cookies

Ingredients:
- 1 *c* butter, softened
- ¾ *c* sugar
- ¾ *c* brown sugar
- 2 eggs
- 2 *tsp* vanilla
- 2¼ *c* flour
- 1 *tsp* baking soda
- ½ *tsp* salt
- 2 *c* chocolate chips
- optional:
    - 1 *c* chopped walnuts

Method:
- Preheat oven to 350°F.
- Cream butter, sugar, and brown sugar until fluffy.
- Add eggs one at a time, then vanilla; mix well.
- Whisk flour, baking soda, and salt.
- Add dry ingredients to bowl and mix until just combined.
- Stir in chocolate chips (and nuts if using).
- Drop rounded spoonfuls onto baking sheet.
- Bake 10–12 min or until edges are golden.
- Cool on rack.

Pfeffernüsse

Yield: about 24 cookies

Ingredients:
- ½ *c* molasses
- ¼ *c* honey
- ¼ *c* butter
- ¾ *c* sugar
- 1 egg
- 2¼ *c* flour
- 1 *tsp* baking soda
- 1 *tsp* cinnamon
- ½ *tsp* cloves
- ½ *tsp* nutmeg
- ½ *tsp* ginger
- ½ *tsp* allspice
- pinch black pepper
- powdered sugar for rolling

Method:
- Preheat oven to 350°F.
- Heat molasses, honey, and butter just until melted; cool slightly.
- Stir in sugar and egg.
- Whisk flour, baking soda, and spices.
- Add dry ingredients to wet mixture; mix into firm dough.
- Roll into balls and place on sheet.
- Bake 10–12 min.
- While warm, roll in powdered sugar.

Linzer Cookies

Yield: about 24 sandwich cookies

Ingredients:

- ¾ c butter
- ½ c sugar
- 1 egg
- 1 *tsp* vanilla
- 1½ c flour
- 1 c almond flour
- ½ *tsp* cinnamon
- ¼ *tsp* salt
- raspberry jam (filling)
- powdered sugar

Method:

1. Preheat oven to 350°F.
2. Cream butter and sugar.
3. Add egg and vanilla; mix.
4. Whisk flour, almond flour, cinnamon, and salt; add in.
5. Chill dough 1 hour.
6. Roll out and cut rounds; cut centers in half of them.
7. Bake 8–10 min.
8. Dust tops with powdered sugar; fill bottom cookies with jam and sandwich.

Shortbread Cookies

Yield: about 24 cookies

Ingredients:
- 1 *c* butter
- ½ *c* powdered sugar
- 2 *c* flour
- ¼ *tsp* salt
- 1 *tsp* vanilla

Method:
1. Preheat oven to 325°F.
2. Cream butter and powdered sugar.
3. Add flour and salt; mix to soft dough.
4. Press into pan or roll and cut.
5. Bake 18–22 min until pale golden.

Gingerbread Cookies

Yield: about 24 cookies

Ingredients:
- ½ *c* butter
- ½ *c* sugar
- ½ *c* molasses
- 1 egg
- 2½ *c* flour
- 1 *tsp* baking soda
- ½ *tsp* salt
- 1 *tsp* cinnamon
- 1 *tsp* ginger
- ½ *tsp* cloves

Method:
1. Preheat oven to 350°F.
2. Cream butter and sugar.
3. Add molasses and egg; mix well.
4. Whisk dry ingredients; add in.
5. Chill 1 hour.
6. Roll and cut shapes.
7. Bake 8–10 min.

Coconut Macaroons

Yield: about 24 cookies

Ingredients:
- 3 *c* shredded coconut
- ¾ *c* sugar
- 2 egg whites
- 1 *tsp* vanilla
- pinch salt

Method:
1. Preheat oven to 325°F.
2. Mix coconut, sugar, egg whites, vanilla, and salt.
3. Scoop rounded spoonfuls onto sheet.
4. Bake 15–20 min until golden.

Biscotti (Almond or Chocolate Chip)

Yield: about 24 biscotti

Ingredients:
- ½ *c* butter
- 1 *c* sugar
- 2 eggs
- 1 *tsp* vanilla
- 2 *c* flour
- 1 *tsp* baking powder
- ½ *tsp* salt
- 1 *c* almonds or chocolate chips

Method:
1. Preheat oven to 350°F.
2. Cream butter and sugar.
3. Add eggs and vanilla.
4. Whisk dry ingredients; add.
5. Stir in almonds or chips.
6. Shape into 2 logs; bake 25 min.
7. Slice and bake 10 min per side.

Vanillekipferl

Yield: about 24 cookies

Ingredients:
- 1 *c* butter
- ½ *c* sugar
- 1 *tsp* vanilla
- 1 *c* almond flour
- 1½ *c* flour
- powdered sugar for coating

Method:
1. Preheat oven to 350°F.
2. Cream butter, sugar, and vanilla.
3. Add almond flour and flour; mix.
4. Shape into small crescents.
5. Bake 10–12 min.
6. Coat warm cookies in powdered sugar.

Italian Ricotta Cookies

Yield: about 24 cookies

Ingredients:
- ½ *c* butter
- 1 *c* sugar
- 1 *c* ricotta
- 1 egg
- 1 *tsp* vanilla
- 2 *c* flour
- 1 *tsp* baking powder
- ½ *tsp* baking soda
- ¼ *tsp* salt
- Glaze:
    - 1 *c* powdered sugar
    - 2–3 *tbsp* milk

Method:
- Preheat oven to 350°F.
- Cream butter and sugar.
- Add ricotta, egg, and vanilla.
- Whisk dry ingredients; add.
- Drop spoonfuls onto sheet.
- Bake 10–12 min.
- Glaze cooled cookies.

Thumbprint Jam Cookies

Yield: about 24 cookies

Ingredients:
- 1 *c* butter
- ½ *c* sugar
- 2 *c* flour
- ¼ *tsp* salt
- 1 *tsp* vanilla
- ½ *c* jam

Method:
- Preheat oven to 350°F.
- Cream butter and sugar.
- Add vanilla, then flour and salt.
- Roll dough into balls.
- Press thumb into center; fill with jam.
- Bake 12–15 min.

Chocolate Crinkle Cookies

Yield: about 24 cookies

Ingredients:
- ½ *c* oil or melted butter
- 1 *c* sugar
- 2 eggs
- 1 *tsp* vanilla
- 1 *c* cocoa
- 1½ *c* flour
- 1 *tsp* baking powder
- ¼ *tsp* salt
- powdered sugar for coating

Method:
- Preheat oven to 350°F.
- Mix oil, sugar, eggs, and vanilla.
- Add cocoa, flour, baking powder, and salt.
- Chill 1 hour.
- Roll into balls; coat in powdered sugar.
- Bake 10–12 min.

Rugelach

Yield: about 24 cookies

Ingredients:
- 1 *c* butter
- 8 *oz* cream cheese
- 2 *c* flour
- Filling:
    - ½ *c* sugar
    - 1 *tbsp* cinnamon
    - ½ *c* raisins or nuts
    - optional:
        - ¼ *c* jam

Method:
- Combine dough ingredients; chill 1 hr.
- Mix filling ingredients.
- Roll dough into circles; spread filling.
- Cut into wedges; roll from wide end.
- Bake at 350°F for 18–22 min.

Mandelbrot

Yield: about 24 pieces

Ingredients:
- ½ *c* oil
- ¾ *c* sugar
- 2 eggs
- 1 *tsp* vanilla
- 2 *c* flour
- 1 *tsp* baking powder
- ½ *tsp* salt
- 1 *c* nuts or chocolate chips

Method:
- Preheat oven to 350°F.
- Mix oil, sugar, eggs, and vanilla.
- Add flour, baking powder, and salt.
- Fold in nuts or chips.
- Form logs; bake 25 min.
- Slice and bake 10 more minutes.

Snowball Cookies

Yield: about 24 cookies

Ingredients:
- 1 *c* butter
- ½ *c* powdered sugar
- 2 *tsp* vanilla
- 2¼ *c* flour
- ½ *tsp* salt
- 1 *c* finely chopped nuts
- powdered sugar for coating

Method:
- Preheat oven to 350°F.
- Cream butter and powdered sugar.
- Add vanilla, flour, salt, and nuts.
- Roll into small balls.
- Bake 12–14 min.
- Roll warm cookies in powdered sugar.

www.ingramcontent.com/pod-product-compliance
Lightning Source LLC
Chambersburg PA
CBRC091135130526
44582CB00034B/173